The Xenophobe's®
guide to the
POLES

Ewa Lipniacka

Oval Books

Published by Oval Books
335 Kennington Road
London SE11 4QE
United Kingdom

Telephone: +44 (0)20 7582 7123
Fax: +44 (0)20 7582 1022
E-mail: info@ovalbooks.com
Web site: www.ovalbooks.com

First published by Ravette Publishing, 1994

First published by Oval Books, 2000
Updated 2002, 2004
Updated and revised 2006

Editor – Catriona Tulloch Scott
Series Editor – Anne Tauté

Cover designer – Jim Wire, Quantum
Printer – Gopsons Papers Ltd.
Producer – Oval Projects Ltd.

Xenophobe's® is a Registered Trademark.

Cover: a Kraków crib.

ISBN-13: 978-1-902825-40-3
ISBN-10: 1-902825-40-3

Contents

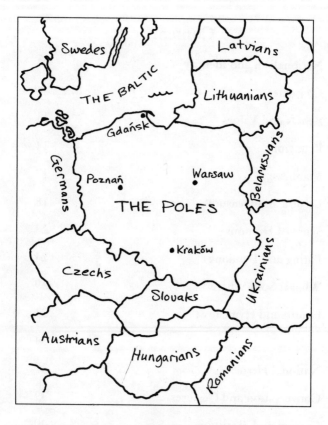

'Geopolitics is the chief architect of the Polish character.'

The Polish population is 38 million, compared with 9 million Swedes, 82 million Germans, 10 million Czechs, 5 million Slovaks, 10 million Hungarians, 47 million Ukrainians, 3¾ million Lithuanians, 149 million Russians, 50 million English, and 300 million Americans.

Poland is 1½ times the size of Spain, a bit smaller than Germany, but could fit into Russia 54 times.

Nationalism and Identity

Forewarned

Legend has it that one fine spring morning in the Dark Ages, three Slavonic brothers, Czech, Lech, and Rus, set out to find new homes. Czech founded the Czech nation in the first good clearing they came to. The other two carried on until Lech saw an eagle building its nest, took it as a sign from the gods, and founded Gniezno, the first capital of Poland. Rus travelled on.

Lech's choice must rank with the ten worst decisions in history. Most of Poland is a flat open plain described by military experts as an 'ideal spot for a battlefield' (a feature exploited today by rental rather than invasion, for NATO manoeuvres, amongst others). Poland has been fought on or over at some time or another by virtually every country in Europe and by some beyond, including Sweden amazing as that may seem, and for whole centuries at a time it disappeared off the map altogether.

But the past is another country. Today Poland is vibrantly independent and planning to stay that way. The only invasions it anticipates, or hopes for, are from tourists.

How the Poles See Themselves

The Poles are self-critical; they know themselves inside out, warts and all. What is more, they will compulsively pick at their blemishes. There is not a problem, be it social, political, economic, national or local, which is not regularly and minutely dissected, put together again in every order imaginable and argued over endlessly. There is no national characteristic, real or imagined, which has not been lamented, and its consequences listed. But when it comes to transferring the words into deeds – well, that is the trouble with Poles: argumentative, undisciplined, no

1

follow-through, straw fire, as any Pole will tell you, interminably. However, this is a game only the home team can play. They would rather not have their faults pointed out by others. Under attack, they will defend every flaw, usually beginning with the phrase, "But you couldn't possibly understand, the problem is so Polish." Persist and you will offend and, with a Pole, taking offence comes only too easily, although luckily it doesn't last long. The most perfect solutions to all their problems more often than not are arrived at late at night, with alcohol fumes heating the air, but are forgotten with the hangover in the morning.

How They See Others

Slavonic brotherhood notwithstanding, the Poles have always considered that East is East and West is best and the twain meet on Poland's eastern frontiers. If money talks, then what it tells the Poles is to travel west when seeking fame and fortune because to the east lie lands which are rich with people who are poor and can't afford Polish plumbers.

Their Russian neighbours are seen as a dull lot, a people born to be dominated, neither enterprising nor hard working, their successes being put down to sheer weight of numbers and ownership of essential raw materials. Although fearful of the Russian mafia, on whom they lay the blame for the astronomic rise in the crime rate, Poles were quick to capitalise on the opportunities that trade with Russia and its former empire offered and many a fortune was made. Unfortunately, as many were lost. The Russian market has always been tricky. Poland is no longer part of the Russian empire and the cold it catches when Russia sneezes is less virulent, but with Russia's stranglehold on world resources, economic dependency is growing, as is Polish resentment.

On their other side, Poles find the Germans a dull lot who, left to their own devices, will stay in their own backyard and nurture *Heimat*, but as a nation are expansionist and (whether by war or trade) are born to dominate. Many a Polish fortune has been made by trading with the Germans. Many a Polish night has been wasted worrying about a German take-over. There are few jokes about the Germans, and the army of Polish migrants in Germany keeps a low profile.

The Poles have the misfortune to be sandwiched between these two giants and try to turn it to their advantage by playing business partner to either and middleman to both. But then they're adept at dancing on tightropes.

For nations to admire, Poles look further afield. Currently, in search of style gurus, they turn to Italy, and not for the first time in history. Bona Sforza, wife of Zygmunt the Aged, introduced the Renaissance to Poland, along with architects, artists and craftsmen, and revolutionized Polish cuisine by bringing lettuce, leeks, cabbages and cauliflowers with her. In the 18th century, Bacciarelli and Canaletto painted Warsaw which was being remodelled by, amongst others, Italian architect Dominic Merlini. After World War II, Canaletto's paintings were used as a guide for the reconstruction of streets and façades that the Germans had demolished.

For centuries the Poles, especially the aristocracy, hero-worshiped the French. Their style was copied in all things, from language to fashion, and anyone who could afford to lived in France rather than Poland. Poles who fought bitterly to save themselves from becoming Russians or Germans voluntarily made themselves imitation Frenchmen. Napoleon was revered, though he only saw the Poles as cannon fodder, and Polish law and many civil institutions are based on the Napoleonic code. But French xenophobia has brought the one-sided love affair to an end. Relations are so frosty that even the French language is rarely taught in Polish schools.

Nowadays it is the English who have captured the Polish imagination and hearts – with their legendary tolerance and sportsmanship and fabled stiff upper lip. Visiting English soccer hooligans dented this ideal – the English are not supposed to be like that – but didn't put them off. There are more 'perfect English gentlemen' in Poland than in the British Isles, and signs in English over shop doors, English pubs, English products, English language schools. Britain and Ireland are among the few countries where the Poles can be employed legally, so they flock to work, study and play in such numbers there has been an explosion of new, budget airline routes.

Poles admire the Americans for their single-minded pursuit of wealth, but see them as *nie kulturalni* – a signal condemnation in Polish eyes. American 'Polish' jokes have little currency in Poland. Poles laugh at Polish Americans, however, and see them as a naïve lot, but put this down to the effect of living in America.

For all that the Scandinavians are just across the Baltic and frequent ferries ply merrily between them, there seems to be little bonding of souls. Shoals of Poles go to Sweden and Norway to augment family finances by fruit picking and the like, and Swedish companies turn to Poland for cheap labour and designers – though Poles are shy about the former and the Swedes are loathe to admit to the latter. Only now has the founder of IKEA admitted that his fortune (and fondness for vodka) came from sourcing his flatpacks in Poland in the 1960s. Not that any of this generates heat. A placid indifference reigns on both sides – a phenomenon amongst neighbours. They share the Baltic, but little else. Oil and water just don't mix.

Of their smaller neighbours, political expediency is leading to a burial of the Polish/Ukranian hatchet. The Lithuanians are tolerated, and in fact usually liked, although sadly the feeling is not always mutual: the two shared a government for too long, with the Poles as senior partner. The Czechs are considered too Germanic, cold and lacking in soul to be proper Slavs. The street cred they earned by choosing a playwright for president is spent. On the other hand, the Slovaks, with whom the Poles share the Tatra Mountains, are well liked.

However, it is the Hungarians who the Poles treat as brothers, although they are not Slavs at all. Though they share neither border nor language, or possibly because of this, Hungarians are seen as kindred spirits who share their aspirations, temperament and love of strong drink.

How Others See Them

The Poles have always been seen as mad romantics. For this read 'manipulable hotheads' – all too often true. Winston Churchill stated: "There are few virtues that the Poles do not possess and few mistakes they have ever avoided." Quentin Crisp went further by describing the Poles as: "Not a nation, but an unsound state of mind."

Before the Second World War, the Poles were considered to be 'Middle Europeans'. After the War, the country itself having shifted considerably westwards, Poles were known as 'East Europeans'. Since the fall of the Berlin Wall and the newly found independence of the Baltic States, Poland, without moving an inch, has become Central European again.

It is hardly surprising, therefore, that many people have no idea where Poland is. Some confuse it with Holland. Many imagine it as permanently snow-bound, presumably associating it with the North Pole.

Most of the West see the Poles as a workforce on the move, a nation of remittance men. Individual countries view this as an opportunity or a threat, depending on how realistic they are about their own skills' shortages. Cause or effect, who knows, but the countries which have slammed their doors shut to the Poles are not doing as well economically as those who welcome them.

Character

The Defensive Pole

Geopolitics is the chief architect of the Polish character. The Poles, famed as magnificent fighters, are in reality avid self-defenders. They would much rather not have to be. Even in its brief period of expansion in the 15th century, Poland acquired territory by treaty, not battle, huddling together with Lithuania against the Teutonic Knights (Prussians by any other name).

Polish xenophobia is a self-defence mechanism: essential to the Poles' survival is the obsessive nurturing of language, culture and traditions, all of which are portable and can be handed on 'underground'.

Polish borders are a thing of such infinite fluidity that geography teachers are rumoured to have a special salary supplement for the extra hours of preparation they have to put in when establishing how many countries border with Poland at any given time, and which rivers are in or out. This also explains why more Poles live outside Poland's borders than inside. Many were left behind during border shifts – like the little old lady who, when informed that her home was now in Russia, not Poland, said, "Thank God, I couldn't have stood another of those cold Polish winters."

Some were reluctant tourists, a long-standing favourite trip being 'Siberia by cattletruck'. Some were washed out by the tides of uprisings or war and deposited wherever. For example, the Poles in France are relics of the 19th-century uprisings, and the Poles in Britain were stranded after the Second World War, hence the Ealing or Bradford Poles.

Now that the Soviet Union is no more, Polish communities have emerged from all its former territories as far afield as Kazakhstan, and former Polish towns like Lviv in the Ukraine and Vilnius in Lithuania. Poland has ever been a net provider of economic migrants and many made for the Statue of Liberty along with every other hungry European. The biggest urban concentration of Poles today after Warsaw is Chicago. There are sizeable Polish communities in Germany, Brazil, Peru, anywhere – in fact, you can't travel far in the world without bumping into a Pole. This means that today's Polish citizens are inveterate travellers, not on package tours but on family visits. Exiles from all over the world, even unto the third generation, flock to and from Poland bent on business and pleasure, delighted that all those Saturday mornings spent learning Polish are paying off at last.

Regional differences in Poland are often still dictated by the national characteristics of the 18th-19th century occupants of the region. Hence Poznań, once ruled by the Prussians, is seen to be home to a law-abiding and industrious people, fanatically tidy and too pedantic for words who, infuriatingly, always turn up everywhere on time. Kraków and its environs are full of petty bureaucrats, like their old Austrian masters. And in Warsaw and district you will find sloppy layabouts, quite like the Russians, in fact.

The regional minority held dear by all Poles, and butt of affectionate 'straw-chewing yokel' jokes, are the Górale, the inhabitants of the mountain regions. The story is told of the Góral who, watching a towny doing his morning press-ups in front of his tent, declared that he had never before known a wind so strong that it blew a woman from under her mate.

The Flexible Pole

It is not surprising that key national characteristics are adaptability, a knack for improvisation, and the ability to make the best of what is available. A good Polish cook is one who can make gourmet soup from a rusty nail. Older Polish cook books give recipes of the familiar 'take a dozen eggs' variety alongside recipes for 'what to use if you have no…'. For example, 'Almond cake if you have no almonds (use ground beans and almond flavouring)'.

Although the economic imperative for these characteristics, known collectively in Polish as *'kombinowanie'*, has gone, relegated to the history books along with the queues and shortages which gave birth to it, it is still an integral part of the Polish personality. A heady mix of cerebral gymnastics, technical skill, gung-ho can-do-ery and a pinch of deviousness, it enabled the Poles to rig up clever devices when there was nothing suitable on the market. It also showed them how to circumnavigate the unworkable the regulations and laws which communist governments created to confound their citizens.

You might have thought that these tactics would fade without the necessity to keep them honed. Not a bit of it. Poles now employ all their stratagems on the E.U.

Poles Apart

The Poles are either positive or negative. They work or they play. They are useless at the sort of playing at work which passes for industriousness in many Western European offices.

At the moment, Poles are divided between those who want to embrace the West, with everything that brings and entails, and those who would defend to the death the essential purity of Polishness (whatever that may be); those who feel that the Church should have a big say in government and those who think it should have none. The quintessential Polish dilemma is that two opposing views can be held simultaneously in one and the same Polish breast. They are either bubbling with life, or comatose; they love or they loathe. It is this total commitment to the occupation of the moment which earns them the reputation of being mercurial. As Hemar wrote in his song: 'If only Poles did systematically and economically what they do spontaneously, they would be perfect.'

The Public Pole

Polish people are very public spirited. They consider it a moral duty to pass comment loud and clear on anything of which they may approve or disapprove. Thus, if you are in a public office tangling with bureaucracy (par for the course, as this is what bureaucracy is for in Poland), you will have a chorus of support from all other members of the queue. If you dawdle at a shop counter, you may have to endure comments on your ineptitude, lack of sense, morals, taste, and so on, from the folk behind you. Public officials and shop assistants will join in, on your side or the other, depending on their mood.

Any minor disaster which may befall you in public will be treated as street entertainment by the audience which will gather instantly. Exhibitionists, this is the nation for you. There is good reason, too, for the thick net curtains which adorn windows. It is an attempt to maintain some semblance of privacy. But it is a vain attempt. There is no defence against intrusion. You need some form of light relief during the long winter nights, so you might as well give in and join the gossip circuit. It is the only chance you may have to correct a few of the wilder assumptions about your innocent life. It also means you always have a shoulder to cry on without the need to explain: people will know before you do what you are crying about.

Style

All – well, most – Poles are born with a sense of style. Even when resources are scant or non-existent, Poles manage to look stylish. This was most evident in the 1960s, when Warsaw shops were full of utility clothing yet the streets were thronged with a fashion parade to rival Carnaby Street or Montmartre. Only the right labels were missing, because the outfits had been run up on the home treadle sewing machine.

During the Second World War, in Palestine, Polish officers who had escaped from occupied Poland were incorporated into the British Army. Within days, they were transforming the standard issue British Army tropical baggy shorts into natty little bum-hugging numbers.

The handful of Polish officers on horseback who hurled themselves at a Panzer division might have been suicidal, but what a stylish way to go. It captured the popular imagination and created the legend of the romantic Pole – all the more surprising as the incident is of questionable authenticity. Devotion to style pervades all areas of life: the table might be rickety, but it is covered with a snowy tablecloth and decorated with a vase of flowers.

The very first periodicals off the starting blocks in capitalist Poland were the style magazines: in fashion, in the garden, in the home. They thrived then and they are thriving still. Now Polish names can be spotted throughout the international style industry, from Ewa Lewis to Tomasz Starzewski.

The supreme example of Polish style is the stylish gesture. Who else would start a revolution with a logo? 'Solidarność' (Solidarity) is a logo so successful that it ranks alongside Coca-Cola and Kelloggs for instant recognition worldwide, and with a style so convincing that it swept Mrs Thatcher, supreme hater of trade unions, into supporting one. Yet not a penny was spent on promoting it.

And on a personal level, just when you are most exasperated with a Pole for yet another promise unfulfilled, a deadline unmet, a late arrival, or sheer thoughtlessness, you will be disarmed by a stylish apology: an unexpected, perfectly judged gift and a nosegay of melting charm. How can you not forgive?

Beliefs and Values

Wealth

Poles didn't used to hunger for wealth and status chiefly because, under Communism, neither was possible or even allowed without major compromise of personal values; and even before that, historically, any self-respecting Pole avoided "trade". The Polish economic miracle has astonished the world, but not as much as it has surprised the Poles themselves.

Yet perhaps it should not have been so startling. Under Communism every Pole had learned how to horse trade to get by. Directors on delegations, engineers on training courses, tourists on coach trips, students on exchange visits, all excursions abroad were seen as an opportunity to bring back goods unavailable in Poland and, as currency could not be taken out of the country, had to be paid for by barter. It was valuable training. As the last few years have proved, being duff at business was not so much a national characteristic as a national inferiority complex.

Status

Despite the Soviet years of brainwashing about classless societies, the Poles still aspire to gentility, and books on heraldry are sold out overnight. Historically Poles were either gentry, and mostly impoverished, or peasants (there was no official middle). In many cases, the only distinction between the two was a gentrifying coat of arms.

But when it comes to actual culture, it is the peasant traditions, dances, and art that are cherished and kept going. Some people can still perform a *Krakowiak* or a spirited *Mazurka* and most have an impressive repertoire of folk songs.

Poland has never bestowed titles of honour on its citizens. All counts, princes and lords have been so honoured by other nations, although Poles are not averse to using such titles. Instead, liberal use is made of academic or professional titles, in conjunction with *Pan* (Mr) or *Pani* (Ms), which are compulsory until you formally transfer to the more familiar *ty* (you). So if you admit to belonging to the medical profession, you will be addressed as 'Pan Doktor', or 'Pan Profesor' if you are an academic. 'Pan Profesor Doktor' is not uncommon, along with other amalgams even more absurd. You could even be called 'Pan Inżynier' if you inadvertently put B.Sc. after your name. ('Inżynier' – Engineer – means you have a university degree, and not that you have come about the boiler.)

The habit of most invaders of lining up the intellectuals against the wall and shooting them makes it surprising that anyone still wants to be one. But Poles do, in droves. So, if you know it, flaunt it. Everyone in Poland loves a know-all and specialists of whatever variety are lionised.

The way to obviate the pitfalls of formal v. informal address (the 'you/thou' problem) is to drink a *Bruderschaft* – a procedure you approach only after you have downed at least half a bottle with the partner you are bruding your shaft with. You sit opposite each other, as for arm wrestling, with a glass in your right hand, you cross arms, and then try to get the contents of the glass into your mouth rather than down your front. The passion of the kiss which usually follows is a matter of the taste of at least one of the participants.

Hospitality

The old Polish tenet of 'A guest in the home: God in the home' still holds good, and most Poles view hospitality as a sacred obligation. Given the acres of still uninhabited terrain and the weather, this is probably a good thing. However, more recent cynical versions such as 'A guest in the home: a pregnant wife', or 'A guest in the home: God knows what for', might be an indication that it is all wearing a bit thin.

Another tenet, still observed, is, 'Get into debt, but be a good host' which can be a source of bewilderment for guests. Even in times of shortages or hardship, Poles laid a table which had visitors disbelieving reported economic realities. Polish hospitality has a way of leaving guests embarrassed with *richesse*, and hosts eating up leftovers for a week. When Poles cater, they cater for a battalion.

Courtship and Marriage

Polish men and boys (including small ones) still kiss women's hands. This can be, but isn't necessarily, an integral part of flirting. The dashing young man nuzzling your fingers could be just signalling that he thinks you old and respectable rather than fanciable.

They also hold doors open, light cigarettes, carry bags and generally behave in a way that we are told the English gentleman behaved before the feminists got to him. It is, of course, Polish women who ensure their men remain gentlemen, by the scruff of the neck if necessary. Polish New Man must wash dishes and push the pram.

The men may flirt outrageously, but not in the florid, poetic, but sadly unconvincing manner of the Latin. Your eyes won't be compared to diamonds, when you know that they are quite piggy. Instead, your new hairstyle or weight-loss will be noticed, your new outfit admired. You will believe him and feel wonderful, yet beware. He might still respect you in the morning, but he will poodle off home to his wife or mother all the same.

The women are just as skilled at flirting; in fact, both sexes, young and old, consider it an art.

Most Poles end up marrying other Poles, and most remain monogamous. In cafés and restaurants, for reasons which remain obscure, couples tend to sit side by side, not opposite each other as in Britain. Most Poles can dance – tangos, foxtrots and polkas – and do so cheek to cheek; steps, that is, not vague swaying shuffles, even at discos.

To be addressed as "little fish" or "little frog" (though, unlike the French, not "little cabbage") should not be cause for concern. These are well-established terms of endearment, and mean your partner loves you dearly, but cannot pronounce, or has temporarily forgotten, your name.

Should he or she take you home to meet mother, size up the family carefully. If you decide to settle in Poland, with the astronomic price of housing and shortage or affordable accommodation, you might be living with them for a long time, as might your children and their spouses. Granted, by then, the older brothers and sisters and their families might have found flats of their own, and one of them might have taken grandma – but don't count on it. The divorce rate is one of the lowest in Europe, but this may be because many divorced couples still have to live together.

Behaviour

The Family

The Poles extend their families like elastic. Cousins are frequently called brothers and sisters, and being 'cousins' can encompass a broad spectrum of relationships.

Such relationships not only mean more at table, they mean obligations if needs arise, in both directions: favours given and received. A careful eye is kept on the well-being of other family members in case they can be tapped for something.

If, on meeting, you are told that "You look well", especially by someone of your own sex, check the bathroom scales. This is the code for "You have put on weight". The obverse, "You don't look well", meaning "You have lost weight", is usually only said by those of a wider girth who are simply jealous, or by mothers.

Polish mothers view all humanity in the same way that the residents of Strasbourg view geese – there for the fattening. If a Polish mother tells you that she has a problem child, it does not mean that little Tomek has burnt his school to the ground and is being sought by the police of five counties. It means he hasn't eaten his dinner.

The Elderly

Changing times and galloping inflation have been unkind to the Polish pensioner. The post-war generation, which worked hard for the secure old age it was promised, now faces an eroded pittance. It is only habit and the continuing economic necessity of extended family living which mitigate the stark reality of mass pensioner poverty. Happily the Poles still need grandmas and grandfathers to look after their young and most children feel obliged to house or subsidise their elderly parents. Furthermore, although financially pensioner power in Poland is negligible, respect for the elderly has not waned.

If you are a cantankerous old person, Poland is the place for you. You can loudly criticise any youngster foolish enough to stand near you, whether related to you or not. You have priority everywhere, as of right. You can prod the largest, most obnoxious-looking punk on the bus with finger or umbrella, and he will vacate his place without a murmur. The pregnant, and those festooned with children, can do likewise. If you are too shy to prod, just look sufficiently old and helpless, and fellow passengers will prod on your behalf, accompanied by a chorus from every other senior citizen in sight.

Children

Not mothers, but mothers-in-law are expected to bring up grandchildren (especially those whose parents are abroad), and often run the households of their working children-in-law. The Poles love children, especially babies, coo over them even in public, take them everywhere and spoil them so much that it is surprising how well behaved most of them are. Few children are sent away to boarding school, although most are sent to camp with the scouts or other youth organizations, or to relatives in the country, to give them a chance to run wild during summer holidays.

Parties are family affairs, encompassing everyone from Great-Aunt Josephine to the smallest infant. Even childless adults have the young underfoot so often that they know how to deal with them, and children quickly learn just how far they can push the adults and get away with it.

Animals

Given the unbelievably cramped living conditions, which still prevail in the tower blocks, it is hard to understand why urban Poles choose Alsatians and Dobermans as pets and not Chihuahuas, or why they have pets at all. The general rule seems to be: the smaller the flat, the larger the dog, with the exception of Kraków where citizens keep miniature dogs – but this is attributed to their legendary meanness.

In rural areas, however, pets work for a living and keep rodents down and intruders out (depending on the species), or they are out of job, house and home.

Other animals are safer in Poland than elsewhere. The Bieszesady forest on the eastern borders is home to primeval trees and exceptional wild-life (including bison and wild boar). Almost a quarter of the world's stork population nest on Polish trees, roofs and telegraph poles, which means that every fourth stork is a Pole.

Manners

Stylish manners are a matter of course. Offering seats, opening doors – all are done with a flourish, though much of this is making an art form of a necessity, for woe betide the Pole who falls below the standard of behaviour decreed by the most vocal custodian of public morality in the world: the Polish grandmother.

Polish grandmothers have taken upon themselves a heavy burden: they have to ensure that their grandchildren, their neighbours' children, indeed the children of the nation – of whatever age – sit up straight and pass the salt just so. All this while simultaneously spoiling them rotten.

The nation's children stay out of their grandmother's way whenever they plan to infringe the morality code. Luckily, grandmothers were young once too. The priest listening to a string of men's names listed by a quavering voice from the confessional was finally stung to ask "But how old are you, granny?" "Eighty-three." "And you still carry on like that?" "No, but it's so nice to remember."

In winter you are expected to remove your snow-laden shoes before entering the house. There is usually a row of slippers by the front door, but since they are rarely of a size to fit your feet, Poles remember to put on clean, hole-less socks when going visiting. Most homes have parquet floors to keep people in training for the harsh, icy, slippery winters. Museums and galleries refine this talent by insisting that you wear felt slippers over your shoes to protect the parquet floor (and polish it at the same time). The sensible intending visitor to Poland puts in a few hours at the local ice-rink before setting out.

Greetings

The Poles are very tactile, and kiss and hug at every opportunity. The standard greeting of either sex for those who are more than casual acquaintances is the bear-hug, followed by a touching of cheeks, with a simultaneous kiss blown skywards, as practised by Soviet diplomats at airports just before they disappeared for good. It is customary to bestow three air-kisses per person greeted.

For acquaintances of a lesser order, the handshake suffices but is obligatory. Everyone shakes hands with everyone, and progress along any high street is impeded by batches of greeters. Lounging teenagers have a strange, sideways, arm-outstretched, 'I'm being very laid back here, you understand' handshake. Solemn small boys make it look like the initiation rite to the Black-Hand Gang.

Never shake hands with a Pole as you cross a threshold – it will bring bad luck to both parties and to the house. Always remember to build handshaking time into meetings. A group of ten newcomers meeting a group of ten locals builds up to a lot of handshakes, and before you know it, it's time to go home.

Leisure and Pleasure

Going Out

The Poles are avid theatre-goers, and the fare on offer is generally reasonable. Not all of it is sombre avant-garde although fringe theatre often takes the physical form of the tonal surrealism of the composer Penderecki.

The Łódź Film School attracted students from all over the world and churned out so many of them that the credits of virtually any film made anywhere in the world list at least one Polish name.

People also love going to the opera and concerts and prefer to go in evening dress; they sit up straight and say "Shhh" at the faintest crackling of sweet papers should anyone be so shameless as to take sweets in with them. Poles sit up straight and say "Shhh" even at informal open-air concerts.

Staying In

From having the most politically repressed, dire television in the world, Poland has progressed to having the most liberal, dire television in the world. However, viewers can hop between two public and countless commercial channels. 'Commercial' equates to 'subscription' and the Poles do subscribe. Satellite dishes sprout from every roof.

When foreign programmes and films are shown, they are neither dubbed nor sub-titled but translated simultaneously in an excited semi-whisper. One translator, usually male, reads all the lines as if every home came equipped with its own private prompt booth. In addition, the original sound track is not turned off, merely down: a conversation going on in the background which viewers try to keep up with in vain. This lends an air of urgency not necessarily related to the action on the screen.

Polish news bulletins are read at breakneck speed as if newscasters were being paid by the word. The tone is more cosy than authoritative, almost like listening to remarkably well-informed neighbours gossiping. One sociologist called them "soap operas for men". Coverage is comprehensive, from all parts of the country and abroad. They are justifiably popular and regularly top the viewing charts. The public channels are deemed to be the more creditable. The logic for the order of items, the length of time devoted to each, and indeed their inclusion at all, is elusive and appears to be regulated by serendipity, rather than by planning.

Polish weather is one of the few relatively stable elements in the nation, and weather forecasts suggesting that it would be worth taking an umbrella are usually right. They, too, are in the mass viewing bracket.

Parliamentary proceedings are televised, with the predictable effect that the Polish powers-that-be are even less respected than before. Scandals, particularly political ones, eat into air-time: interminable parliamentary investigations are transmitted live and whole and are savoured with great gusto by viewers. No-one makes such a meal of scandals as the Poles.

A cheap way of filling broadcasting hours is the street interview. The Poles, delighted to be asked for their views, gladly step forward. There are opinion polls on virtually every aspect of Polish life: market research has come to town in a big way, but though the format delights, no-one has quite figured out what the object is, or indeed that an object is needed.

Children's programmes, on the whole, are good. Presenters talk in normal voices, and guests are not dunked in green slime. A long-standing tradition is the 'goodnight story' at 7.30 p.m., the signal for the nation's parents to try to pack youngsters off to bed.

Unlike the Western version padded with celebrities plugging something, Polish chat shows, in the land where the specialist is king, are full of specialists, talking about what they specialise in. Game shows, however, are as vapid as elsewhere and reality TV as pervasive.

The Church, previously excluded, fills all residual televisual space; Mass and other religious ceremonies are not just reserved for Sunday viewing.

Much of the rest of Polish scheduling is the usual pap of international soaps and serials. These are a fairly accurate barometer of the state of the nation's finances. The older the episodes of American or English soaps and serials, the worse the state of the national economy. Homegrown soaps are popular and are in the British or Australian tradition – everyday lives of common folk – though they tend to feature more middle, than working, classes. To satisfy the persisting requirement for sagas about the exciting lives of unbelievably rich folk, Poles import South American soaps. These go out at an earlier time and are aimed at women are cooking dinner, to take them away, at least in thought, from the kitchen sink.

Outings

In a country which has one third of its land covered in forests, no Pole is more than a bus ride away from one. Love of the forests lies deep in every Polish heart. They are a source of food, recreation, exports, and, if the worst comes to the worst, a bolt hole if an invader becomes too obnoxious.

The Polish countryside has a characteristic patchwork quilt appearance. Poland was the only country of the Eastern block that avoided land collectivisation and as there is no *jus primo geniture,* property is willed to all offspring equally. Thus sizeable estates could degenerate after a few generations into tiny strips consisting of two rows of beans, three of potatoes, etc., with two porkers and a cow tethered in the middle, all on less land than the average European farmer sets aside.

This process is now in reverse. As rural unemployment has emptied the villages, the remaining farmers have expanded and automated and the patches on the quilt are growing in size and changing the landscape. The horse and cart is not yet the picturesque anachronism that it is elsewhere in Europe, neither is the back-bending hand-picking of crops, but it is the tractor and combine harvester which are now becoming the norm. Fortunately, the old fertilising ways have not yet died nor agri-business taken hold, so it has been relatively easy to revert to healthy organic farming.

Poland is one of the few countries in Europe that still has a self-proclaimed peasant class. Indeed, there is a peasant nestling in the heart of even the noblest Pole.

Just as all sensible Poles ensure they have a member of their kith and kin in every country they wish to visit, so they also kit themselves out with several near and dear ones tilling the land somewhere in Poland. It ensures that urban dwellers have fresh organic produce and the kids have some grass to run around on. Those lacking the foresight to have families in the country take advantage of the growing agro-tourism industry (invented to combat rural poverty) or invest in *działki* (allotments). The latter are beautifully tended, with a staggering array of crops and the Polish allotment shed, far from being a hotchpotch of rusty corrugated iron, is a palatial miniature house. The effect from a distance is of enchanting garden estates for pixies. Poles who live in tower blocks spend their weekends, summer holidays and even retirement in them.

Sports

The most popular Polish leisure-time activities are mountaineering, hill walking, sailing and skiing – all of which the sporty can indulge in without leaving the country.

The most popular national sport of recent years has been watching Adam Małysz, world class ski jumper, tiny by name (Małysz means 'little 'un') and by nature (5'5"), and cute with it. His success won the nation's heart and spawned a raft of new talent keen to imitate him.

Given their fondness for winter sports, it is surprising that there are not more such success stories. One reason they hark back to communism with justifiable nostalgia is sports provision. The scholarships and training facilities which were available to all talented youngsters then have melted away in the heat of capitalism. Private sponsorship is still too rare.

The Poles are too anarchic to be team-game minded. If they must play team games, they choose volleyball or basketball. But they love their football: once they have found 22 volunteers (or better still, 11 to pit against 11 from another nation), the populace can sit back in its armchair and indulge in epic bouts of criticism. This is why bridge is the national participative passion. It gives scope for the players to argue with both partners and opponents alike.

Sense of Humour

The tone of most Polish humour is wry, dry and frequently black – a form of whistling in the dark in bleak situations – and Poles see all public figures, particularly those in the political arena, as legitimate targets; after all, no-one ordered them to run for office. A party of senators is touring an art gallery and the curator points out the works of various painters. "Is that a Picasso?" asks one, as they all peer at it. "No, that's the mirror."

Political satire, or the great Polish Political Joke, which under Communism was a substitute for political life is, if not actually dead, then in hibernation. Current targets are social mores and lifestyle, both in the process of monumental change. Hence corruption, still rife in the medical profession, is the butt of this joke: Doctor: "Yours is a very rare case which will enrich medical science." Patient: "Will 20 *zloty* be enough, doctor?"

Poles tell jokes against themselves – thus beating others to it. For example: the manager of a travelling theatre complained that when he put on tragedies the takings were comic, and when he tried showing comedies, they were tragic. Or, as a chat-up line, the self-deprecating: "Why didn't you come into my life 20 kilos ago?"

As for subject matter, curiously for all the awfulness of Polish plumbing, scatology features less in Poland than it does in France or Italy. But sex does, as do mothers-in-law:

"So what does your son-in-law do?"
"Exactly what I tell him."

Fashions in humour come and go, but little Jasiu, scourge of the nursery, is ever precociously young. He even has his own web site.

Teacher: "Jasiu, your homework is so good now. Has your father stopped helping you with it?"

Jasiu: "Can 5 year-old Basia be pregnant?"
Gynaecologist: "Of course not."
Jasiu: "The rotten little blackmailer."

Jokes involving drunkenness are legion:

"Excuse me, what time is it?"
"D'you know, I could do with a drink too."

Wife: "You promised you'd change into a different man."
Husband: "I did. He drinks too."

"Life begins at 50 (50 grams is the standard measure
    of alcohol)."
"It's even better at a 100."

Diary of an Englishman:
Monday: I went drinking with some Poles.
Tuesday: Hangover so bad, I almost died.
Wednesday: I went drinking with the Poles.
Thursday: If only I'd died on Tuesday."

Religion, too, features in jokes, and with a uniquely
Polish irreverent twist:

Confessor to young man: "So how do you sin?"
Young man to confessor, "Father, I came here to confess,
    not to boast."

Priest: "Children, what must we do before the priest
    can absolve us of our sins?"
Little Jasiu: "Commit them, Father?"

Poland is one of the few places outside Britain where
whimsy and nonsense are popular. Hence the cartoon of a
wingless bird flying through the air and thinking: "Why do
I need a fridge when I haven't even got a phone?"
    Puns abound, e.g:

"I read one of your poems."

24

"The last one?"
"I hope so."

In the battle of the sexes, both are in flux, on a complementary roll of self-doubt and rudderlessness. As usual in Poland, doubts are turned into jokes:

> After a major row with her spouse, a wife is soaking away her ire into a soothing bath. Emerging from the foam she looks in the long mirror: front, side, back, deep sigh, other side and then front again. Another deep sigh, followed by an explosive: "Well, serve him bloody well right!"

Eating and Drinking

The French live to eat, the Poles eat to live. Food is thought to be a failure unless plentiful – nouvelle cuisine would never get past a Pole.

Polish food was designed to be filling. It took account of the cold, hard winters and sheer physical energy expended in daily living. The climate is still the same, but office life is decidedly less calorie-intensive than tilling the soil and gathering the harvest. Most traditional Polish cooking was heavy on preparation time as well as on the stomach, but doctors are busy explaining how heavy it is on the heart, too, and meals are finally shrinking.

Breakfast, taken at an ungodly hour because work starts early, is a selection of cold cuts of meat with bread and coffee. 'Second breakfast' is whatever you can get away with at work: usually another coffee and a sandwich at your desk, and if your desk happens to be in the front office of a bank, you munch in full public view.

Work finishes around 3 o'clock, and the main meal of the day, *obiad* (dinner), is eaten as soon after as transport home allows. Soups as a first course are obligatory and substantial, and look as if they should be tackled with knife and fork. The most famous is *barszcz*, or beetroot. *Rosół* (chicken soup), as in the Jewish tradition, is said to be more than a soup: it is the medical and psychological equivalent of the English cup of tea.

For the second course, 'meat and two veg' is the norm – pork, beef, chicken, but not lamb. The Poles equate sheep with mutton, which they declare (not unreasonably) smells. The alternative main course is pasta: dishes like *pierogi*, triangular sweet or savoury ravioli, known throughout Eastern Europe and universally, though wrongly, translated as dumplings.

Kolacja ('cold-cuts'), the last meal of the day, eaten any time between 6 p.m. and midnight, depends on the sleeping (or otherwise) habits of the family. Like breakfast, it consists mainly of bread, cheese, and cold meats. This is not as monotonous as it sounds for Poles have a bewildering variety of cold meats. They will smoke anything, and have as many varieties of sausage and hams as the French have cheeses.

The Poles love cheeses too and produce many and smoke some. The unique native cheese, *oscypek*, doubles as folk art – diamond shaped with folksy pattern embossed on it. It comes in two forms – soft and fresh, like dehydrated curd cheese with a salty tang, or hard and gratable, not unlike parmesan. They also market a bewildering range of creams, especially soured: for soups, for deserts, for sauces. Think of a culinary need and Poland produces a cream to fit.

Of traditional dishes *bigos* is usually rendered on menus as hunters' stew. Historically, *bigos* was made in a cauldron over a camp fire in the middle of a forest in winter. Hunters would arrive with a pot of sauerkraut and, adding to it whatever they had managed to bag, simmer it for several days, interrupting the process with spells of cooling it in the snow. Today, a low hotplate replaces the camp fire and the fridge makes do for the snowy wastes, but two days' cooking is still the recommended minimum. This is a good way of waking up jaded appetites on the third day of Christmas, and one of the best disguises for turkey left-overs.

The Poles pickle things – a throw-back to long, hard winters before refrigerators – gherkins, beetroot, cabbage, onions, mushrooms, anything. Most housewives have an atavistic urge to pickle something come the autumn. And if they don't pickle it, they preserve it in alcohol. Traditional Polish herbs are parsley, marjoram, bay leaves and masses of dill. Polish pickles are exported all over the globe and now everyone has learned that pickled cucumbers taste better with a sprig of dill in the bottle. Supermarkets now offer a dazzling variety of seasonings and there is every sign that the next generation of Poles will grow up believing, along with other young Europeans, that curry is their traditional national dish. However, the Polish fight-back campaign is in place, with a marketing strategy so effective that Polish food is now available all over the world. *Kabanos* (pencil thin sausage) or *bigos* could be set to become the new curry.

Polish snails are not eaten, but collected and then packed off to France for the French to eat, a superior way of throwing them over the garden fence.

Compôtes and cakes feature heavily, especially a sort of Swiss roll filled not with jam, but with ground poppy seeds mixed with dried fruit (figs, dates, raisins) and honey.

Fish, when it makes an appearance, is either pickled (herrings) or freshwater: carp, pike, salmon, trout. Though the Polish fishing fleet is one of the largest in the world, Poles have never quite taken to the fruits of the sea. When the government tried a poster campaign to overcome this, their slogan 'Eat cod' acquired the graffiti: 'Shit tastes even worse'.

The fruits of the forests, however, are held in high esteem. Berries and mushrooms of all sorts are collected avidly, and the most urbane of townspeople will know their nuts.

If you get marooned on a desert island, choose a Pole as your companion and you will never go hungry.

Drinking and Toasts

Breakfast coffee in many countries is a weak and milky affair. Not so in Poland where it consists of a generous spoonful of ground coffee heaped into a glass of boiling water. If your spoon does not stand up on its own, it is a failure. Experience teaches you when to stop sipping, just before you swallow the grounds.

Tea is also taken without milk, served with lemon in a glass specially designed to ensure that you burn your fingers. Tea with milk is known as 'Bavarian' and considered only fit for breast-feeding mothers.

Vodka used to be consumed at home, which was only fair since much of it was brewed there. A child's chemistry set, described on the box as 'The Little Chemist', is still known as 'The Little Brewer'. However, the bars and pubs springing up in even the littlest towns are tempting many to wine and dine al fresco and in public.

Vodka is divided into two types: dry and clear for the men, theoretically at least (and this includes Bison vodka with the blade of grass in it), and sweet for the ladies. Beware Polish liquors. They are usually 40+% and drunk undiluted: firewater. The women might be seen to be sweeter toothed, but their heads have to be just as strong as the men's.

Technicoloured sweet vodkas can be made of virtually anything: ripe morello cherries, honey, nuts, lemon, hot chilli peppers. There is even one with bits of gold floating in it. Those Poles who do buy their vodka in a shop often doctor it at home and create delicious home-made liquors. These are generally made with a base of Polish pure spirit, 90%, 180° proof, the nearest to pure alcohol possible, and the strongest drink known to man. Avoid drinking this neat without prior instruction and a soft landing.

The methodology of drinking is in tiny cut-crystal glasses, drained in one gulp, after a toast, and usually, sensibly, accompanied by lots of food. The Pole who, invited home by an Englishman, sent his host's treasured Waterford flying into the two-bar electric fire is apocryphal. Poles hang on to their glasses to ensure refills.

Rounds of toasts usually start with the health of the hosts, followed by the health of the guests, followed by the health of the beautiful ladies, and the handsome gentlemen, then bachelor days. After that, tradition leaves each dinner party to its own devices. The uninventive can always continue with endless repetitions of the formula, and toast "The health of the guests" for the nth time – for as long as they have strength to lift a glass.

What is Sold Where

There are shops and shopping centres in Poland which would not look out of place in the chic quarters of any Western capital city. The multi-nationals have discovered Poland and have forced grey out and bright colours in. Though luxury goods, of course, have matching price tags, there is a growing elite who can afford them.

Even the average Pole has undergone a change of lifestyle. Now that there are no shortages, and the plural of 'man' is no longer 'a queue', free time has doubled. People stroll around the streets or sit in cafés instead of having to wait in line, and there is no need to tote spare carrier bags and large amounts of cash at all times, just in case.

These days Poles wheel trolleys round Western-style supermarkets and buy what they want when they need it. A queue is what you frighten your children with when telling them stories of long ago. Along with tales of dragons, you can tell the joke about the disaster when the queue to Gum in Moscow collided with the queue to Smyk in Warsaw*. And if they still won't go to sleep you can tell them Mrożek's tale of the bruhahah when a shop acquired a stock of suits of armour which customers fought to possess, though none had any idea what use they could put them to. Or you could show the very jacket you bought in 1984 in the butchers in Olsztyn, next door to the jewellery shop where you bought a kilo of sugar after queuing for four hours in the snow.

A whole generation of children has never witnessed empty shelves and meat queues and their parents are happy for them. But when the kids are in bed and it's nostalgia time, many still have the odd pang of longing for the days when life was young and happiness was a kilo of ham, twelve rolls of lavatory paper or a bra which actually fitted, and everyone in the queue – the great leveller – was equal.

The times when virtually all goods in shops had instructions in every known language but Polish are also gone, and with them the guesswork: "Is it a tube of mayonnaise or hæmorrhoid cream?" International branded goods now have Polish labels or at least overprints, and many have advertising campaigns geared specifically to the Polish market. After all, there are 38 million Poles inside Poland and another estimated 32 million beyond its borders, thus beetroot soup has found its way on to the multi-national's menu along with other Polish tastes and needs.

Polish producers have also improved their marketing and packaging by employing the considerable native graphic skill. Make-up containers and vodka bottles are a particular delight. However, quaint anomalies remain to amuse the intrepid shopper, such as signs announcing that the shop sells leather goods when from the contents it is clearly a florist. But this springs from the bewildering speed of change brought on by capitalism and its atten-

*The word for 'queue' in Polish also means 'a local train'.

dant evil – bankruptcy. Ask for the way to a shop and passers-by will point and add, "Well, at least that's where it was yesterday."

A more sinister cause of the occasional disappearance of shops or indeed whole buildings is the 'mafia', or more correctly in Poland, the mafias, who have been known to bomb or burn down the unco-operative. As one satirist recently explained: "Before there was one mafia, and everyone knew who, where and why: it was the Central Committee of the Communist Party*. Now there's the Wołomin mafia, the Pruszków mafia, visiting mafias from over the border…"

Health and Hygiene

Most Poles are amazingly well-informed hypochondriacs. Not only will they tell you in great detail exactly what is wrong with them and how their ailments are being treated, if you don't stop them in time they will also tell you exactly what you should be doing about all yours.

The Poles tend to specialise in one complaint, and not only will they know more about it than many a Western professor, they will be best friends with, or related to, the most eminent specialist in the country, who they will quote extensively.

Polish doctors do not seem to mind being accosted with medical queries at parties or in public places, and will happily agree that your manifestation of the disease is the most interesting they have ever come across. The ultimate example of this was the doctor passing through a cemetery who was accosted by a voice from a grave

---

*One of the cherished ironies of post-Communist Poland is that the Polish Stock Exchange, symbol of capitalism, is housed in the former HQ of the Central Committee of the Communist Party.

asking for a cure for worms.

The Poles' knowledge of treatments will encompass the oldest herbal remedies and the latest Western drugs. It is worth listening – they are usually right. Medi-centres, equipped with the latest technology, flexible appointment systems and, as private health care goes, comparatively modest fees, have sprouted all over Poland. The Poles frequent them as regularly and as often as they go to church. They feel compelled to keep their finger on the pulse, and while they're at it, check up on their blood pressure, cholesterol, insulin levels, kidney efficiency – anything and everything that can, and therefore should, be measured.

The place to get hold of the potion you have been recommended is one of the new pharmacies which were amongst the first shops to be upgraded. Where many hospitals are still rather grubby, sad places, most drug stores have floors you would not mind eating off and where the light bounces off every gleaming bottle and ampoule. On sale are the products of the world's leading laboratories alongside every alternative medicine known to man. If a queue is to be found anywhere in Poland, it will be here, as the pharmacist advises customers at length and expertly on anything which might be ailing them. Queuers seldom complain – they are too busy eavesdropping.

For those too busy to haunt their local pharmacy, health products dominate television. Well over half of all advertising time is taken up with them, with those purporting to cure the short and long term effects of alcohol leading the fray, followed by palliatives for the ravages of old age such as herbs to cure fading eyesight and, of course, rejuvenating creams. Much of the other half of viewing time is taken up with financial contrivances such as insurance to pay for all these nostrums.

Europe-wide statistics for mortality and the length of wait for operations place Poland above the U.K., to the delight of one and the disbelief of the other. Even so, if you have to go into hospital, make arrangements for your meals to be sent in or prepare to go on an unscheduled diet. Be prepared too, to bribe the doctor, nurse and cleaning lady. If you don't, you could find yourself in a corridor with a dust sheet over you. Tackling bribery in the heath service has proved to be one of the most obdurate targets for reform.

Best by far to stick to the less lethal diseases and the private clinics which, having given you a print-out of the state of all your internal organs, should this be unfavourable, will provide the names and consulting times of the leading specialist in your chosen affliction. Or carry a big purse.

Running Water

Polish handbasins have no plugs because the Poles wash in running water. Basins and baths all have mixer taps so you are not scalded, and the hot water supply usually runs off the local generating station. It used to be free, and is still cheap.

Away from home the wise carry emergency lavatory paper with them. Public plumbing though improving by leaps and bounds can still be, well, basic. W.C.s are staffed by formidable ladies who will, in exchange for a pre-ordained sum which is usually marked on a piece of cardboard somewhere near their person, hand over a solitary piece of grey lavatory paper, splinters optional.

The Atmosphere

The popular explanation for most woes in Poland is pressure. This does not mean stress, though if any people can justifiably claim to be stressed, the Poles can. This is the atmospheric variety. '*Ciśnienie*' is chanted mantra-like

33

as the basis for any number of ills, from varicose veins to the state of the economy. High and low blood pressure sufferers alike claim to be ruled by the barometer, and there is no such thing as a Pole with normal blood pressure.

High blood pressure sufferers will quote, ad nauseam, the latest health warnings about the damage their bodies are undergoing, but they will never act upon them. Thus: "I shouldn't really be eating this, but…" is the general refrain. Low blood pressure sufferers knock back cups of coffee which would make a horse reel, without apparent ill effect, explaining that it is the only way to keep their circulation going.

Culture

Literature: Publish and be Overwhelmed

Writing, be it in the form of newspaper, periodical or book, is the vein through which Polish life blood (i.e., words) flows. It is axiomatic that three Poles on a desert island will form four political parties (of which two will be coalitions and one a splinter group) and each will have its own newspaper, journal and series of occasional publications.

Behind every writer lurks a publisher, and behind every publisher an archivist. Libraries mark the presence, or even the mere passage, of Poles throughout the world. The Standing Conference of Polish Libraries Outside Poland has representatives all over the globe.

A Polish house is not a home without its bookcase, and one shelf will be devoted to the classics, more often than not Henryk Sienkiewicz, the Polish Walter Scott. Known abroad by *Quo Vadis* rather than by name, he was translated into English and published by an American with the unlikely name of Jeremiah Curtin. One of the first international best-sellers on a modern scale, his works were (and still are) repeatedly filmed, but he earned little from them because of Poland's copyright laws, or rather, the lack of them. Beloved for his *Trylogia* set in the days of Poland's glory in the 17th century, many Poles can and do recite whole chunks of him.

Another *sine qua non* of every domestic bookcase is Adam Mickiewicz, a revolutionary Romantic, exiled with Chopin and others after the November Revolution of 1830 to Paris, where he penned wonderfully evocative descriptions of the Poland of his childhood:

'Fatherland, you are like health itself. Only he knows your true worth, who has lost you.'

His early works still have power and relevance: the 1968 Warsaw students' revolt started at a performance of his play *Dziady*. His epic poem *Pan Tadeusz* has been filmed by Wajda, and a few random stanzas of this run:

One happiness remains: when evening greys,
You sit with a few friends and lock the door,
And by the fireside shut out Europe's roar,
Escape in thought to happier time and tide,
And muse and dream of your own countryside.

That land forever will remain as pure
And holy as first love; unmingled sure
With faults remembered or with hope's distraction
And unchanged by the moving stream of action.

A more recent addition to the classic canon is Wisława Szymborska, 1996 Nobel laureate for literature. One of her poems is entitled *Conversation with a Stone*. Another simply states:

The joy of writing
The power of preserving
Revenge of a mortal hand.

Music

For a nation with modest, popular, musical ability, Poland is home to a decent array of world-class composers and musicians, from the ubiquitous Chopin, through Paderewski (inter-war President and proof positive that Poles are better off ruled by musicians than electricians) to the acquired tastes of modernists Lutosławski and Penderecki or the more traditional Górecki.

Polish pop music, though a feeble mirror of Western fashion with occasional flashes of originality, is experimenting with a fusion of folk, especially Góral music, and reggae, which seems to work surprisingly well.

Poland never gave up on jazz even when the rest of the world did, so Polish musicians are now leading the international jazz revival.

Architecture

The Poles not only defend the historical centres of their cities from the passage of time and progress, they lovingly rebuild the depredations of others less sentimental. After World War II, they recreated Warsaw and Gdańsk. However, though there are medieval towns with façades as yet unspoilt by McDonald's arches, much of Poland is now lit up with neon.

Neo-brutalist Soviet architecture was an even greater disaster than the aberrations that reigned in the West, and its heritage of serried ranks of heavy, concrete blocks of flats march across the landscape. Attempts to jolly up their façades are testing Polish ingenuity but with some measure of success. Those old houses that were not knocked down were left to rot, so the only alternative was self-build. Few models were allowed, all with the same boxy, flat-roofed silhouette which every owner now feels dutybound to modify – their roof-lines swoop rollercoaster-like as neighbour outdoes neighbour.

New homes range from the tasteful to the ridiculous, from Le Corbusier to Dallas-style haciendas – and everyone is at it. Even mouldering ruins are being bought up. The whole country is an enormous building site.

National Heroes

It is ironic that many of Poland's most famous sons and daughters went by non-Polish-sounding names and are therefore often not immediately associated with the country at all. France is the fiercest counter-claimant: Chopin had a French father and surname, but his upbringing, heart and prominent nose were Polish. In Poland he is known as Szopen.

Marie Curie-Skłodowska, discoverer of radium, was all Polish. The non-Polish element of her name came from her husband, Pierre Curie, and the Poles are fighting a rear-guard action with the Marie Curie Foundation to get them to incorporate the name she was born under into its name. Copernicus (Kopernik in Polish) was a Pole from Polish Toruń. The Germans who claim that as the town was from time to time German and therefore so is Copernicus, are treated as vexatious litigants and just plain silly. The Swedes, during their excursion into Polish lands, looted Kopernik's library, and it is now in Uppsala. Their excuse for hanging on to it – that Poland is unsafe because everyone keeps on looting it – makes a warped kind of sense.

More people associate Kosciuszko with a mountain in Australia than with a Pole who fought for Polish and American independence. Few non-Poles know that King Canute was half Polish as was Bonnie Prince Charlie (both on their mother's side). Conrad wrote in English and anglicised his name, and who can blame him? Would he have been as widely read if he'd been published under Korzeniowski? Tit for tat, Poles make sure that any foreigner entering a Polish library catalogue becomes a naturalised Pole, so Shakespeare becomes Szekspir, and Winnie the Pooh turns into Kubuś Puchatek.

In Poland itself the only way to ensure continued popularity is to be dead. Then your portrait will be hung everywhere and streets will be named after you.

The Communist heroes who were forced upon the nation have been expunged from signposts, maps and pedestals, and the old heroes reinstated, but there has been no revenge-taking on even the most hated of the old guard. The joke that had General Jaruzelski asking his portrait what will become of them both, and receiving the answer, "They'll take me down and hang you instead", has not come true. The Poles are not vengeful by nature. Nor do they seek out feet of clay in their chosen heroes, but forgive them their minor peccadillos.

What they cannot forgive is heroes who let the side down abroad. Wałęsa was given a long rope. The Poles were always aware of his limitations and just crossed their fingers and hoped that he'd get by in foreign palaces, but when he turned pompous and pretentious with it, he became the butt of a legion of jokes.

Leszek Balcerowicz, architect of the Polish economic miracle in the eyes of the international banking world, is another matter. A brilliant economist, he is liked as a person but loathed as a financial reformer. But then, prophets are never popular at home.

Popes, especially if they are Polish, are the exception that proves the rule. Even those who are not sure whether they believe in God believed in 'their' Pope. Where Wałęsa was Poland's maverick son who could not be trusted to remember which knife to use and when, Wojtyła was the clever one who could always be relied on to talk intelligently and hold his own amongst foreigners, however posh they might be. As for holding idiosyncratic views on sex, well, even heroes are allowed the odd foible or two. Every Pole with a valid passport who could fight their way on to a plane or coach headed for Rome for the Papal funeral. The rest made for key places within Poland and mourned as they watched on giant TV screens: the last chance for the nation to reflect in the glory of the man, and start the campaign for the making of the saint.

Conversation and Gestures

On average, the Poles gesticulate a bit more than the French and a bit less than the Spanish.

A number of signs convey that you are just about to seek alcoholic sustenance (such as pinging your throat with a flick of your thumb and forefinger), or that the other fellow has already done so, far too liberally. If your shaggy dog story is met by a palm held waist-high, first face-down, then face-up, your audience is telling you that when they were 'so' high, the joke had a beard 'that' long.

Many sayings translate exactly from Polish into English. "Small beer" is *małe piwo* which is 'small beer' – though why this should be so it is difficult to say. 'Wolf' is cried in the same way, and 'dear' has the same double meaning of 'beloved' and 'expensive'. However, some sayings are improved in the Polish version; for instance, the enigmatic English: "Don't teach your Grandma how to suck eggs", is rendered more graphically in Polish as: "Don't teach your father how to make children."

The words *"Na zdrowie"*, literally 'to your health', are said for 'cheers', but also as 'bless you' when someone sneezes. Small boys with runny noses who haven't got a hanky say out loud: "King Sobieski had a moustache" (sleeve rubbed under the nose), "and a long sword" (sleeve rubbed downwards along the trousers).

Most anatomical references are directly translatable. The commonest 'soft' swear-word (the equivalent of 'shit') is *"cholera"* – presumably from the time it was endemic, which fortunately it no longer is. *"Ale jaja"*, literally "what bollocks", is said more in admiration than condemnation, for example in response to a good tall story.

There are some in Poland who can swear entertainingly for an hour without repeating themselves, but this ability seems to be linked more to professions than to nationality: troopers, plumbers and doctors lead in this skill.

The questioning of the victim's paternity, the virtue of his or her mother, and graphic descriptions of what can be placed where, are the most popular themes. The fad for using *"kurwa"* (whore) as a punctuation mark is an egalitarian trend used by doctor and dustman alike, and mainly, though not exclusively, by males.

Custom and Tradition

Religion

An old truism claims that Poles believe not in God, but the Madonna. Certainly the Marian cult is strong: there are many more pictures and statues of her than of the rest of the Holy Family, and in 1717 she was even officially crowned Queen of Poland.

The nation has a pragmatic attitude to religion. There is a church or place of worship somewhere in Poland for virtually every denomination, and a range of sects – from Moonies to evangelists of every hue – is gaining ground amongst the young.

The Poles are decidedly more religious in times of need. They perform the rituals assiduously but only go along with those parts of the dogma which suit them. Hence contraception was never a problem: swallow the Pill, proceed in the usual manner, and then confess all. In good times they treat God much like roué nephews treat spinster aunts – with the odd respectful nod and bouquet as a hedge against future expectations.

When the Communists rather foolishly tried to stop the Poles practising their religion, the churches filled to over-flowing. 'Forbidden' is a term of encouragement to a Pole. Now that this kind of protest is no longer necessary, churches are slowly emptying and, despite the 'Wojtyła factor', will soon be left to old ladies and tourists, just like the rest of Europe.

The increasingly vocal interest (some would call it meddling) of the Church in politics – a battle between Church and state for hearts, minds and power – is turning previously pious folk against the clergy. Perceived clerical greed (priests are battling for state salaries), doesn't help. The anti-abortion legislation, forced through the *Sejm* (Parliament) against considerable opposition, has earned the Church the sort of opprobrium previously reserved for the Communist Party.

Nevertheless, much of Polish social life still revolves round the parish church, for where else can you show off your latest outfit or car, meet your friends for a gossip, or flirt? And most festivals and public life hang on its calendar. It's the pageantry, pomp and circumstance of Roman Catholicism which appeal most to the Poles. Protestantism never stood a chance – much too grey.

Holy Days

Easter is still a religious festival rather than an excuse to block all roads to the coast with a gigantic traffic jam, and worship takes place in church rather than the DIY megastore. Folk wandering around with baskets contain-ing three-course meals are either going to feed their rela-tives in hospital or, if it is Easter Saturday, going to church to have their Sunday breakfast blessed. On Easter Monday the Poles pour water over each other. This is an old custom which reaches back to paganism, and you can come home drenched.

Boże Ciało (Corpus Christi) is an excuse for little girls to air their Communion dresses, before they grow out of them, by parading through the town. In Silesia this parade is held on St. Barbara's Day – she is patron saint of miners; indeed every parish and many occupations have their own patron saint and processions.

Each parish, village and town also has its little wayside shrine, decked out with fresh flowers, even in remote mountain passes and woodlands, often with a plaque to mark atrocities of the recent or distant past.

The top Polish saint is Our Lady. Top shrine is an icon, the Black Madonna of Częstochowa which, like Lourdes, attracts pilgrims from all over Poland, many on foot. When in 1981 the wearing of *Solidarność* badges was forbidden by martial law, the people wore badges of Our Lady of Częstochowa instead. Either that, or electronic resistors – the name said it all – and Lech Wałęsa was an electrician, after all.

At Christmas each Polish church has a crib (*szopka*) and strives and connives to have the best in the neighbourhood. Families trail from church to church to admire and (of course) criticise them. The parish priest of a Wrocław church, an avid collector of clockwork toys, takes over an entire side chapel and his crib marches, nods, bongs and bows in perpetual motion. Kraków cribs are elaborate confections with tiny silver foil figures housed in edifices that echo Kraków's spires and onion domes. They are judged at annual competitions and the best end up as museum pieces. "*Robić szopkę*" (literally "to make a crib"), which elsewhere might conjure up images of a humble stable with shepherds and sheep, is Polish slang for making a fuss.

Christmas would not be Christmas without the

Midnight Mass, when citizens weave their way to church after *Wigilia,* the traditional 12-course Lenten feast. Miracles occur annually: no church has yet spontaneously combusted, despite the air being 90° proof.

All Poles know all the words to the Christmas carols, but sadly, unlike the Welsh, Italians and Russians, they are not noted for their choral abilities. Enthusiasm and volume make up for the lack of vocal talent.

Holidays

The Poles have a fair selection of civic festivals, many in honour of battles, won or lost. Voted top by 60% of the nation is Constitution Day, 3rd May. The Communists tried to supplant this with International Labour Day on 1st May (known in Poland as the Workers' April Fool's Day), when school children and workers were driven into the streets and told to march and wave flags. This bit so deeply into the Polish psyche that it was commonly felt to be the most universal manifestation of oppression. There are recorded cases of dissidents encasing limbs in plaster to avoid attending. However, it goes against the Polish grain to discard any holiday from the pack, whatever its origin, so by way of compromise many Poles now celebrate from the 1st to the 3rd of May.

With their usual enthusiasm for finding new ways of celebrating anything, Poles are taking to commercial festivals like ducks to water. Totally unknown until a few years ago, Valentine's Day has taken off like a rocket. Fuelled by flower vendors and card manufacturers, St. Valentine should be appointed the patron saint of commerce. Even the Post Office joins in by issuing special stamps with hearts or roses.

Children's Day is marked by a day off school. Most schools arrange a programme of visits and outings, and the children are allowed a certain amount of behavioural leeway. They do not as yet receive presents on Children's Day. What with birthdays, name-days, St. Nicholas (6th December, when presents appear under pillows), Christmas, Holy Communion and Confirmation, Polish children do well enough already. Parents thank heavens that they don't know about the tooth fairy.

Deaths

Deaths are announced in newspapers, on black-edged posters pinned to walls and trees in town centres and on the front gate These can either give the time and place of the funeral, or they can be 'In memoriam'. Funerals are widely attended and death is, logically enough, the second most popular topic of conversation after health.

On the gate to the cemetery in Zakopane is the motto: 'A nation is a people and its graves'. The Poles revere their ancestors and 1st November, All Souls' Day (otherwise known as National Traffic Jam Day), is celebrated all over Poland. Families trek from one end of the country to the other, and even come from other countries, to visit family graves, and they spend hours planning elaborate itineraries to fit everyone in. The glow from the candles in larger cemeteries can be seen for miles.

Cemeteries are almost never empty. Families tend graves as carefully as they do their front gardens and the tombs of well-loved national figures, especially children's authors, are regularly visited and decked with school badges, flowers and candles. Some tombstones are real works of art. Sometimes schools and scout groups are given a cemetery to look after, in particular the graves of families who have died out or moved away.

Several cemeteries, such as Powązki in Warsaw, where the dead of the Warsaw Uprising lie, are national monuments. The simple crosses, with inscriptions such as 'Soldier, aged 14', are unbearably moving.

Bearing Gifts

Instead of birthdays, the Poles have the very civilised habit of celebrating name-days. This has several advantages:

a. Calendars give the day's saint which reminds you who you should ring or visit.
b. No-one asks your age when it's your turn.
c. If clever or greedy, you can manage two parties and sets of presents a year.

Poles do not hand greetings cards to people with their gifts. Cards are for sending to those you are not in physical contact with. Flowers are for handing to people. Flower shops are everywhere and flowers are bought for name-days, birthdays, anniversaries, greetings, partings, when popping in to see a friend, or just because you feel like it.

On International Women's Day, another former Communist festival, the usual procedure is for men to buy flowers for as many women as they can afford: wife, mistress, mother, secretary, friends; and a bottle of vodka for themselves. The director of a large factory who wanted to please all his women workers allegedly read a prepared speech and then gave a bouquet to each one of the 700 workers on the first shift, but in the middle of the second shift he had a heart attack and dropped dead, thus unintentionally giving the workers the best present of all – the rest of the day off.

Assistants in florist shops the world over are bewildered by the number of men buying big bunches of roses on this day, even handing them out to women passing by. Only Poles know why.

Folk Art

Gone are the days when every home came equipped with a regional folk costume for high and holy days. The network of state support for folk artists, like so much of the Communist infrastructure of subsidies for worthy causes, has collapsed. Yet there are still many towns and villages where, on Corpus Christi or other holy days, over-voluptuous ladies insist on parading through town in the wake of a Madonna or some other icon, as if they were still young maidens. Not all of them do this with an eye to the tourist trade.

Folk art is by no means dead. One way or another, all Polish homes have a little something that is folksy in origin: a *pasiak* (brightly striped folkweave throws from Łowicz), a tablecloth of primary coloured cabbage roses, a teapot or plate displaying customary patterns or even a bookmark decorated with paper cut-out cockerels. The item may be stylised almost beyond recognition, but it will be there, ready to be dragged out for Christmas, Easter, the Third of May or any other occasion, whether religious, patriotic or social, which needs a boost to make it more authentic or more fun.

Poles cling to tradition. Archaeologists examining the stomach contents of a prehistoric bog man found boiled wheat, poppy seeds, nuts and honey, in other words, '*kutia*', an essential Christmas Eve dish from Eastern Poland.

Systems

Banking

Credit, as in borrowing, is a relatively new sport in Poland but one that Poles have taken to like ducks to water, as a recent aphorism shows: "If I didn't have so many debts, I wouldn't have anything." Salaries are paid straight into accounts, most bills can be paid by credit transfer and advertisements for loans are everywhere. Soon the debts of individual citizens will be as impressive as the national debt. It didn't take long.

Green Matters

The Poles are basically a rural nation, and the devastation and pollution caused by Communist industrialisation was deeply felt by the whole population. Much of this legacy has been eradicated, the most toxic industries in the more sensitive areas being the first to be shut down. The golden roof of Kraków's Wawel Castle is no longer pitted by acid fall-out from the foundries of Nowa Huta and even Katowice is cleaner now that so many of its factories and mines lie dormant. However, the aftermath of the U.S.S.R.'s social engineering lives on: Silesia's unemployed have only pure air to consol them.

The Poles had expected that Germany would help in the clean-up. It makes sense that the country into which your pollution flows will be first with assistance. The Germans, however, having their own unified pollution to deal with, were not in position to aid the polluters further upstream until they had resolved the mess further down, illogical though that is in physical terms. And this is not the end of it: beyond Poland's borders lie the even more polluted, radioactive lands of the Ukraine and Russia.

The children of the two worst affected areas are within a few hours' drive of the fresh air of the Tatra mountains. Here they are taken for at least two weeks of the school year to give their lungs a fighting chance.

Transport

Although the Poles travel extensively, they do not believe in travelling light. Only a Pole would try to convince check-in staff at an airport that a microwave constitutes hand luggage, in addition to a large holdall and five carrier bags. Only a Pole would succeed.

If you ask Polish friends what they would like you to bring them as a present, the answer may well turn out to be a gear box or spare washing-machine engine instead of a box of chocolates. They are also quite likely to step off an aeroplane themselves bearing an eight-foot carved wooden shelf (as hand luggage) for you.

The occasional tiny Fiat 126, once the most popular car in Poland, can still be spotted trundling around. Roof rack laden to double its height and twice its length, it warms the heart. It once transported a nation.

The national rail service has undergone a transformation and trains are now clean and on time. They are also expensive and therefore fairly empty, so the authorities have 'discovered' marketing. Free coffee and a biscuit on the express probably costs little to lay on but makes an excellent impression.

Local transport is full to bursting. There are trams in most towns and two-part buses, linked together with rubber concertina affairs. The rear is best avoided, for the whiplash generated by the second half is awesome.

The Warsaw metro, one of Europe's major long-playing transport dramas alongside the Channel Tunnel, is now running a regular service and its users have forgotten the troubles involved. Talk of extending it to a network is seen as a sensible proposal – albeit a long-term one – and not a joke.

Recycling

Rediscovered now by the rest of the Western world, recycling never went out of fashion in Poland for purely economic reasons. As early as the 1970s, Coca-Cola plants were set up with attendant bottling and re-bottling plants and, despite the advent of cartons and plastic containers, glass bottles are still a source of revenue for the nation's children.

The average Polish mechanic can and does construct something useful out of the equivalent of the contents of a Western scrap yard. Poverty sometimes has advantages.

Education

An oft-quoted Jesuit once said: "Give me a child at seven, and he is mine for life." The Polish educational system, like most of the rest of Europe, is based on the Jesuit model, and children start school at seven. So-called 'zero' classes for six-year-olds are gaining in popularity, but the impetus behind them is not so much educational as practical, i.e., the childcare needs of working parents.

Primary education finishes at 14, and compulsory secondary education at 18 when pupils sit the *Matura*. This resembles the French baccalauréat, both in style, with its wide range of subjects, and in the devastating effect it has on the entire family of the sitter.

Starting school comparatively late in life, Poles finish it even later, and sometimes never. Eternal students are numerous. The first university degree you can get is an M.A. or M.Sc., conferred after a five-year course. The next step is a Doctorate, after which come several echelons of even more rarefied Doctorates or Professorships. One can also specialise in each and every subject and all specialists publish papers – endlessly.

The whole educational system, currently beset with the problem common to every other area of Polish life – chronic underfunding – is in a state of flux. Abysmally paid, the teaching profession cannot attract or keep good staff. The shortage of classrooms is so desperate that many children are taught in shifts.

The national curriculum, not so long ago cast in iron, is being smelted down all over the place. Wider ranges of subjects are being introduced alongside new technology though money considerations are slowing down the latter and aspirations have overtaken possibilities. Overheard in a school: "From today children, we will learn mathematics with the help of computers. So, Jasiu, tell me, what is three computers added to six computers?"

In the meantime, educationalists write paper after

paper, and sit on committees in relays, making statements such as: "The programme is too overloaded", or "The programme is too lax". What is offered is restructuring, what is needed is cash. There is a growing private sector but the standards here are no better, not because of lack of cash but because of interfering, bossy parents.

There is also a vast range of private classes in virtually anything – arts and crafts, aerobics, aromatherapy. The most prolific and popular are business, marketing and computers, whether at home or abroad. As employers no longer pay extra bonuses to those with degrees, many young people are choosing to attend such classes rather than go to university. Many do both. The whole of Poland seems to be studying something.

Crime and Punishment

The police force lacks the social kudos and salary structure to attract high flyers and is consequently low in numbers and brain cells. Yet the once inexhaustible well of police jokes has run dry, perhaps because reality beats satire hollow: in a brilliant display of their skills, Warsaw police shot three escaped tigers and a vet.

In international crime tables, Poland features often and high. Warsaw is now in the top ten of the murder league, gang-warfare being the main cause, and the odd passer-by caught in the cross-fire swells the numbers. Poland is also to be found on the 'must see' list of touring drug dealers, especially those whose mind-altering substances of choice are amphetamines.

Much of the luxury stolen car trade passes on its east-ward way from the West. Mercedes are firm favourites amongst the *mafioski* and Merc owners outside the fraternity are almost certain to be periodically relieved of them. Helpful police will direct victims to the man who will, at a price, retrieve the vehicle from the one who stole it. Owners of lesser cars may well find only parts of their cars missing, but the same procedure for retrieval by ransom applies. Poles in full evening dress have been known to take the more 'attractive' parts of their vehicles to the concert to ensure continued ownership of them.

On the Road

Latest statistics place Poland at the top of the 'My traffic jam is worse than your traffic jam' league in a survey that ranks world road congestion. By the end of a hot summer, the weight of the through-traffic bearing both legitimate and stolen goods and Western expertise from West to East, and raw materials and disillusioned bankers and entrepreneurs from East to West, can be seen imprinted on Polish asphalt. Drivers know that they stray from the canyons worn in the tarmac at their peril – or that of their cars' suspension.

The new hazard of an excess of fledgling drivers has combined with the older one of the Polish peasant who views the highway, including motorways, as his own, and is apt to launch out with a horse-drawn cart as laden as Constable's *Hay Wain*, or with a herd of cows, with a careless disregard for life and limb.

A specific hazard on the roads used to be the road police who lurked behind bushes and leaped out in front of the unwary, lollipop held aloft, to exact instant fines (which some treated as pocket money). But gangs of no-gooders have taken to stopping passing motorists to hijack or rob them and the legitimate police have been forced to advise motorists to ignore the lollipop.

Minor offences, such as jay walking, are also punished by on-the-spot fines. Drunk driving is increasing, despite the draconian penalties which start with heavy fines and end with imprisonment, and Polish prisons are no guest houses. Sentient Poles operate rotas at parties. Soft drinks are laid on for those who have drawn the short, sober, straw. Even so, the statistics show that the number of cars and accidents are up a third, year on year. It's not the drunkenness that's the problem, it's the bad driving.

Business

After the economic disasters in Russia and the East, the much-vaunted Polish economic tiger has had to draw in its claws and unemployment figures are high, but the general mood is still buoyant. Young Poles believe that they can achieve anything, if they put their mind to it.

From a standing start in the early 1990s of having virtually no private industry at all, the Poles have managed to open around two million private companies. Many went to the wall a day later. Most were one-man-and-his-dog affairs. Some can now be called "big business". The glass industry was one of the first to be turned around from a cripple into a thriving concern. Today, no self-respecting western store is without pieces of Krosno glass, and lesser glass-making companies send their industrial spies to copy Krosno designs. IBM and Microsoft declared amnesties on copyright in order to stop Polish bootleg software, then established legitimate usage by offering generous discounts. Now many of the world's computer firms assemble and even produce in Poland.

In the shipbuilding industry, where it all began, the Szczecin Shipyard has held its own and is expanding. Bits of the Gdańsk Shipyard still function, but large chunks are being developed into loft apartments for Polish yuppies.

The world's companies are beating a path to Poland, mostly to Warsaw. The unemployment statistics for the capital are very different from those for the rest of the country. At the present rate, the rest of Poland will soon become a dormitory for Warsaw commuters, interspersed with holiday homes.

Unemployment especially in the regions, is rife, so Poles must seek work all over the world and euros, pounds or dollars earned on building sites abroad are brought home to rebuild the private and public infrastructure. Recent guesstimates place between one and two million of the workforce abroad. Real figures are probably lower but, however many, the effect on the national economy is undeniable. At Christmas, when Poles working abroad return to their families to meet, feast, ski and pray, the exchange rate goes down.

The Work Ethic

The Poles, young and old, do not like to be seen at sweaty toil, especially by outsiders. It lacks style. Work should take place between consulting adults in private. However, they always were and still are a hard working bunch. Although state employees might still get away with it, private employers won't tolerate the previously common practice of employees clocking in at their offices but working on commissions for others, so many Poles practise serial employment, racing from one job to another. Then they come home and collapse in a heap in front of the television.

Of course, the tenets of work ethics do not apply to officialdom. As far as the bureaucrat is concerned, papers have to ripen on desks for the prescribed amount of time before they can be looked at, let alone seen to.

Obliging optimists by nature, the Poles want to tell you what they think you want to hear, a fact that is particularly true of estimates of time. Best, therefore, to add anything from five minutes to eternity to the kick off time you are given for social gatherings. It's not that Poles mean to be late, it is just that time's wingèd chariot often overtakes them. This does not apply to work where clock-watching is obligatory, business appointments are kept to the second, and latecomers are told what is thought of them.

Women at Work

Polish women have long been educated alongside men, and there are as many women as men in engineering and the sciences. There are also plenty of women in the upper reaches of most professions, but those dominated by women – for example, teaching, librarianship and nursing – are poorly paid. Two wages have long been economically essential, and as well as going out to work, women still carry the major burden of housework and childcare. Some things are truly universal.

Job Hunting

Jobs in Poland are usually acquired through an elaborate form of patronage. Young people finishing their education scrabble around looking for a job amongst relatives and friends, and get appointed as supernumerary menials, to be promoted from within if they are any good. Every organization has room for supernumeraries, so this presents no problems.

Management skills have arrived, and there are numerous ads for organizations offering to teach interview techniques to both interviewer and interviewee. You can acquire these skills in person at courses up and down the country, or by post, or you can have someone prepare an elaborate CV for you. But as yet few jobs are advertised. The grapevine still rules.

This may explain why Polish business cards are miniature works of art and, after the name, list all the letters of the alphabet in various sequences, to indicate academic or other qualification, affiliation to institutions, marital status, shoe size, hat size... Business cards are handed out by all and sundry to all and sundry from a seemingly endless supply. You can be sure that the delegate still dishing out cards on the last day of a conference, when everybody else's supply is spent, is a Pole.

Pay

When Poles tell you how much they earn, they give their basic salary, rounded down after deductions. They are trying to impress you with the paltriness of what they earn. When Americans do the same, they will quote gross figures, rounded up, to show how well they are doing. This may, in part, account for the Polish opinion of the overwhelming wealth of all Westerners. Any conversation on the subject of salaries soon degenerates into an absurd attempt to represent comparative wages by the numbers of bottles of vodka or loaves of bread and fishes the average road-sweeper can buy in a month.

Government

Generations of Poles were told by their conquerors that they were too inept at politics to be trusted with their own self-governance – the "It's for your own good" excuse for invasion. To ensure they were not infected by foolish ideas of independence, Western borders were also slammed shut, but in vain, as this purported conversation between a Polish president and a favoured actress shows:

"Ask for anything and it's yours."
"Give passports to everyone who wants to leave."
"You flirt, you want to be alone with me."

Nonetheless, over time, the grain of truth contained within the specious argument metamorphosed into a seed of doubt which sprouted into received wisdom. Thus, when the Russian troops went home, the national self-confidence was a little shaky. But contrary to everyone's expectations the economy blossomed.

People still criticise their government with a will, but privately they are grateful that the crass idiots in power are, at last, their own crass idiots in power.

Politics

Following the advice of the leading Western specialists, Poland now has an electoral system which is labyrinthine in its complexity, expensive to administer, and inconclusive, virtually guaranteeing hung or minority governments. Add to this a president with extensive powers of veto over legislation, and political life is one mad whirl of coalitions, partings, and makings-up, like a mad gavotte with the dancers having to improvise the steps. A cabinet reshuffle was described in the press as "one new minister and five used ones".

After communism, the Poles wanted their government to be perfect and much time and hot air was expended in pursuit of this ideal. Few perfectionists remain and a new pragmatism prevails: all the Poles want now is a government whose greed or ineptitude is not so great that it bankrupts the nation. The politicians are being allowed to get on with it while the people concentrate on bettering themselves. Poles take life's changes stoically. The old adage which ran: "We survived capitalism, we'll outlive communism" now in reverse order, coupled with a wry shrug, seems to be a serviceable enough philosophy.

A graffiti writer illustrated what the nation thinks of its politicians. Under a sign in the Gents saying 'Hooks for Members of Parliament', he had added 'Or their coats'.

Language

Pronunciation

Anyone who tells you that the Polish alphabet consists of 's' and 'z' is lying – well, exaggerating. Only half of it does.

Some 'z's are not zeds at all but part of conjunct consonants, like 'sz' or 'cz', pronounced as 'sh' and 'ch' – sounds which resemble a saw slicing through a nail. A dot over a 'z' (ż), or a conjunct 'rz', make another unique Polish sound, like a jet aeroplane taking off.

Other letters in the Polish alphabet created to confuse the unwary are: 'w' pronounced 'v', and a crossed 'l' (ł), scourge of typesetters, pronounced 'w'. Apart from these, there are the various diacritics without which Polish looks naked to a Pole. An acute accent over an 'o' (ó) turns it into a 'u', and over a 'c', 's' 'n' or 'z' softens them, as does an 'i' following it. Little tails on 'a' (ą) and 'e' (ę) turn them into 'an' and 'en' respectively.

There are three 's' sounds – 's' as in 's' and 'ś' as in 'sh' and 'sz' – like bumble bees in bottles. There are also three 'c's. There are reported cases of foreigners managing to pronounce Polish words, but not many.

Teach Yourself

Should you ever express a willingness to learn the language, most Poles will be only too happy to oblige. What they will try to teach you, if you are not careful, is *"Chrząszcz brzmi w trzcinie"* ('a bug is buzzing in the reeds'). The *Guinness Book of Records* reckoned this was the most difficult phrase an English-speaking tongue could pronounce, until it was ousted by a Czech phrase of equal length but even less vowels.

If you still want to master the odd Polish phrase, ask for a translation of words of your own choosing. Even then be wary. The Poles are notorious for trying to teach you the sort of words your grandmother would object to, while insisting they mean 'Good morning'. Should you meet a little old English granny who spouts filth in Polish with a sweet smile, you have met the victim of a Polish wartime airman. Be gentle or you will ruin the romantic image she has nursed for so many years.

Inflections

Polish is a highly inflected language: everything declines and conjugates even more than in Latin. It could be worse: Old Polish had three numbers – single, for one of you, plural for lots, and dual for cosy tête-à-têtes. Luckily this was too much even for the Poles, and was abandoned in the Middle Ages. It is still found only in the sorts of obscure old adages that are best left alone.

One of the spin-offs of inflecting everything is that the order of words is not important – much like the bouffant hair-do it takes hours to get into place, but once assembled, it will take a hurricane to dislodge it. You sort out what is done to whom and why from the case endings. This goes some way to explain the curious order of words pronounced by Poles struggling with the English language and may also explain why, among the groups of immigrants to the United States, they were considered to be slow on the uptake by the others (and thus the butt of endless jokes).

Before you accept some outrageous statement of the 'man bites dog' variety, check if that is really what is meant. It could just be a grammatical misunderstanding and not the sensational piece of gossip you thought it was. Those Poles professing to be 'charming' or 'exciting' are not being impossibly vain, they are just mixing up their active and passive participles.

Where once the Poles would accept no-one's word for anything, the young now take the English words for everything (complete with Anglo-Saxon spelling), and stick them on shop-fronts and in newspapers, much to the disgust of the not so young. Battle-lines are drawn and skirmishes have commenced over such vile imports as 'hamburger' or 'leasing'. But a language that doesn't even have a word for 'filing' or 'sitcom' is fighting a losing battle.

Diminutives

The Poles miniaturize everything and everyone. Every noun, proper or improper has a diminutive. A cat that is just called a *kot*, rather than *kotek, koteczek, kicia or kiciunia,* is a very large cat indeed. A *maleńki stoliczek* expresses five degrees of diminution: *mały* means little; *maleńki* – very little; *stół* is a table; *stolik* – little table; *stoliczek* – very little table. And yet a *malenki stoliczek* is not as small as all that. That would be *maluteńki stoliczek* (teeny weeny table).

Diminutized, all male names seem to end in -ek and most female ones in -sia, regardless of how they started off. Małgorzata (Margaret) thus becomes Małgosia, and is usually known as Gosia, Basia is short for Barbara and Kasia is short for Katarzyna (Catherine). Try calling all the women Ania and all men Krzyś (i.e., Krzysztof – Christopher). You will have a 50/50 chance of success, although increasing numbers of infants are now labouring under improbable and unslavonic names such as Damian, Marlene or Vanessa, rendered into Polish as Damianek, Marlenka and Waneska.

After a round of vodka you don't stand an earthly chance, so if all else fails, remember that most Poles are used to being addressed by foreigners as 'Erm…?' and will magnanimously award you points for trying.

The Author

The Lipniackis arrived in Britain (via Siberia and Palestine) when Ewa was three. Educated in a Polish convent boarding-school in Northamptonshire, she went so far as to take a degree in Polish at London University.

In her late teens she was one of the first English Poles to set out to rediscover the real Poland, and found a vast family stretching from the Wołomin Poles to the Poles of Częstochowa. She has been extending this family web ever since and supplementing it with a network of friends.

A naturalised Willesden Pole, she maintains close links with the Birmingham, Wolverhampton, Rugby and Galashiels Poles. Her home has become a central node on the Polish world trade routes linking the Warsaw, Kraków, Poznań and Gdańsk Poles with the New York, New Jersey, Toronto, Melbourne, Venezuelan, South African and Brazilian Poles. Like bindweed, Polish roots are long and indestructible.

A librarian by profession, she can often be found at the Polish Library in Hammersmith of which she is chairman. She has written several rarefied works on librarianship and a clutch of children's picture books – most of which are illustrated by her cousin, a Balham Pole.